House Beautiful

DECORATING
WITH BOOKS

House Beautiful

DECORATING WITH BOOKS

MARIE PROELLER HUESTON

HEARST BOOKS
New York

HEARST BOOKS
New York

An Imprint of Sterling Publishir
387 Park Avenue South
New York, NY 10016

PAGE 1: Books are frequently incorporated into decorative arrangements in the home. Four volumes chosen for their all-white color scheme add height and visual interest to this still life on the mantel.

PAGE 2: In an antiques dealer's library, the walls and shelving are painted a crisp white to balance the heavy wood furniture, like the walnut drawing table and straight chair, which are both Flemish pieces from the seventeenth century. Brass spotlights and a brass ladder rail frame the top shelf on which bound copies of The Connoisseur form a strong horizontal band of color. The collection of books is arranged with the eye of an artist; volumes stand up, lie flat, and vary in height from one shelf to the next. Precious antiques and heirlooms punctuate the scene.

OPPOSITE: In this writer's work space, his towers of books surround a library table now used as a desk. Arranged in such a manner, the books add to their utilitarian purpose by forming a unique backdrop for the room. Although the placement of books appears random—and a bit precarious—the occupant knows precisely where each volume is and has become adept at slipping one out without toppling the rest. Reference books are kept close at hand atop an old steamer trunk.

PAGE 6: Books can be chosen to underscore a room's color scheme. In this airy living room, brown leather bindings and books in deep hues echo the dark wood and woven furnishings found throughout the space. Placing a few books to either side of each shelf creates a natural frame for prized possessions.

PAGE 8: Built-in bookcases create an unexpected yet striking backdrop for a dining room. Not only are walls of books pleasing to the eye, they're sure to spark conversations in such a setting.

This book was previously published as a hardcover.

Library of Congress Cataloging-in-Publication Data

Proeller Hueston, Marie.
  House beautiful : decorating with books / Marie Proeller Hueston.
    p.cm.
  Includes bibliographical references and index.
  ISBN 978-1-58816-847-4 (alk.paper)
  1. Books in interior decoration. I House beautiful. II. Title.
  NK2115.5.B66P76 2006
  747'.9—dc22

                                    2005018697

10 9 8 7 6 5 4 3 2 1

DESIGN BY PATRICIA FABRICANT

First Paperback Edition 2011

House Beautiful is a registered trademark of Hearst Communications, Inc.

www.housebeautiful.com

For information about custom editions, special sales, premium and corporate purchases, please contact Sterling Special Sales Department at 800-805-5489 or specialsales@sterlingpublishing.com.

Distributed in Canada by Sterling Publishing
c/o Canadian Manda Group, 165 Dufferin Street
Toronto, Ontario, Canada M6K 3H6

Distributed in Australia by Capricorn Link (Australia) Pty. Ltd.
P.O. Box 704, Windsor, NSW 2756 Australia

Manufactured in China

Sterling ISBN: 978-1-58816-847-4

I have always imagined that Paradise will be a kind of library.

—Jorge Luis Borges

[There is] no furniture so charming as books, even if you never open them, or read a single word.

—Sydney Smith, in *A Memoir of the Reverend Sydney Smith*, by Lady Holland, 1855

CONTENTS

FOREWORD

LEGENDARY INTERIOR DESIGNER BILLY BALDWIN ONCE DECLARED, "BOOKS are the best decoration." We couldn't agree more. Set on a shelf or lying open on a table, books become decorative elements in a room, as vital to the overall scheme as any piece of furniture or work of art. We can't imagine any home without them.

Among the countless interiors we've featured in *House Beautiful* over the years, some of the most memorable have been the rooms in which books played a major role. We especially love to see them used in an unexpected way—stacked beside a sofa as a side table, arranged in a dramatic display atop the mantel, or resting on the seat of a curvy side chair.

You'll find a font of ideas, both creative and traditional, throughout *Decorating with Books.* In addition to inspirational photographs, useful tips will shed light on topics such as the best ways to organize a large book collection, the optimal placement of bookcases in a room, the proper care of antiquarian volumes, and much more. May this book become a worthy addition to your own library.

The Editors of *House Beautiful*

INTRODUCTION

"HE THAT LOVETH A BOOK WILL NEVER WANT A FAITHFUL FRIEND," proclaimed the seventeenth-century British scholar, Isaac Barrow. More than three centuries after Barrow's death, his words still resonate with book lovers everywhere. Why do these ubiquitous objects continue to inspire such adoration? One reason is that cherished volumes are like favorite family photographs: Each time you look at them, you are transported back to joyful times. Perhaps you remember the day in grammar school when a literary classic you've now read countless times was first placed on your desk. Holding a dog-eared novel in your hands may conjure up recollections of a carefree college vacation in Europe, while the sight of a glossy museum catalogue can trigger the same awestruck feeling you experienced the first time you saw in person the work of an artist you greatly admire. You may even picture yourself among the shelves of the dusty bookshop in which you discovered an out-of-print tome (at last!) after years of searching.

Besides providing a window on the past, books show the world who we are today. A collection of books gathered over a lifetime reflects its owner's pursuits, pastimes, and passions. No matter what the category—be it fly-fishing, French cuisine, Chinese snuff-boxes,

OPPOSITE: Prominently placed on a table in the center of a spacious foyer, the stacks of books in the entryway inform guests that they are entering the home of booklovers. Four groupings of relatively equal height work well with the round table, and the slight disorder of the arrangement complements the home's casual elegance. A single volume is included in a simple still life on the blue table, continuing the literary theme across the room.

Thick shelving of blond wood and neat rows of books are well suited to modern interiors. Keeping the shelves at an equal height from top to bottom creates a sense of symmetry and acts as a grounding force for the furniture and artwork's curved lines. The home's sunlit corners are ideal spots for a comfortable reading chair.

or English architecture of the eighteenth century—a book on the subject has been published somewhere in the world. This may explain the tendency of bibliophiles to steal a glimpse at the bookcases in a new acquaintance's home. If the topics they find there are subjects in which they have little interest, conversation will quickly drift in other directions. But should those shelves harbor familiar titles, especially obscure ones, a lively discussion will ensue, and, quite likely, friendship will blossom.

Books can also be appreciated on a purely aesthetic level. Consider the leather bindings on antiquarian books—florid, gold-leaf designs still visible after centuries of use, and colors deepened by the handling of successive generations. Beautiful endpapers in bold marbleized patterns, graceful botanical prints, or strong stripes create a sense of anticipation when a front cover is opened and a sense of closure when the last line has been read. Dust jackets brittle with age showcase the fonts, color schemes, and graphic-design motifs popular at the time they were printed. Even the edges of pages have a distinct look about them, whether ragged, gilded, or dog-eared. From small-press editions of poetry to pulp fiction novels churned out in the 1960s, books possess visual and tactile qualities that CD-ROMs and Internet databases can never replicate.

With all these wonderful attributes to recommend them, is it any wonder that so many of us accumulate and surround ourselves with books? Fortunately, we live in an age when all but the rarest volumes are affordable and accessible. This was not always the case. Before the invention of movable type in the fifteenth century, books were painstakingly transcribed by hand and illustrated with precious tinctures and gold leaf. As valuable as works of art, books were more often stored in a lockbox than displayed on a shelf. Even after the printing press made it possible for titles to be published in larger editions, books remained within only the reach of the wealthy—individuals who had both the financial resources to purchase them and the education to know how to read them.

Over the course of the nineteenth century, advancements in mass-production techniques allowed books to be

Books need not be arranged standing up. Here, in this dramatically decorated living room, oversized art, lamps, and books work together to create an eye-catching display. The books are stacked neatly on their sides in a small dark bookcase which helps draw attention to the books themselves rather than the bookcase holding them.

The versatility of books can conform to any decorating taste. Anyone for whom bookcases seem overly structured, for example, can choose to stack books on tabletops, cupboards, and even the floor. In this sunny work space, neat piles top a pair of antique Chinese cabinets and form a tower in a nook beside the window.

printed ever more quickly and inexpensively. With literacy rates on the rise in the industrial world, the burgeoning middle class became voracious readers. Men and women could visit a local bookstore and choose from a wide variety of subject matter: ancient history, epic novels, agriculture, etiquette, and cooking, just to name a few. Thus began the modern quandary: What does one do with books once they've been read? For the upper class, the answer was simple: Rooms designed specifically for the storage of books had been a feature of grand manors for hundreds of years. In more modest homes, bookshelves served their purpose admirably. One wall in a living room was often lined with shelves, while freestanding secretaries were a common sight in bedrooms. Special volumes such as a family Bible or a set of encyclopedias were frequently positioned atop a sideboard or dresser for all to see.

BEYOND SHELVES

When it comes to the arrangement of books in the home, much has remained the same between then and now. Living-room walls are still lined with shelves, secretaries can still be found in bedrooms, and heirloom bibles are still placed on tabletops. There are, however, a few notable changes. To begin with, books are no longer confined to shelves and tabletops alone but might be stacked on an ottoman, piled on the floor, lined up on a bench, or even draped over a ladder. Our concept of a library has expanded to include not only distinct rooms but underutilized spaces like hallways, dressing areas, and alcoves—just as long as those spaces are devoted to books. (This is good news for anyone who's always loved the look of a formal library but never had a room to spare.) The list of rooms considered appropriate for book displays has expanded as well; some of the spots where you might find books these days are dining rooms, kitchens, stair landings, and baths. Although the aesthetic appearance of books has always been part of their appeal, creative decorators and homeowners are now using books as decorative accessories—to add a punch of color to an interior, or as pedestals for objets d'art—without any intention of ever reading them.

Decorating with Books celebrates the myriad ways books are used and displayed in the home today, from traditional interpretations to contemporary visions. On the following pages, you'll enter spacious libraries that exude Old World grandeur, cozy alcoves that invite quiet contemplation, minimalist interiors that showcase modern art, and even a romantic bedroom tucked beneath the eaves. You'll see rooms that shelter thousands of books and those that feature only a few, artfully placed. You'll contemplate neutral color schemes that foster a sense of serenity and palettes that create a sense of richness and luxury, like turquoise, emerald green, and scarlet. What ties all these disparate spaces together? The tangible presence of books has enlivened and personalized each and every one. Whether your bookcases are overflowing or your collection is just beginning to grow, *Decorating with Books* will help you achieve the look that's best for your home.

A low bench placed at the foot of a bed is an ideal foundation for stacks of art books. The simple lines of the arrangement reflect the pared-down styling of this bedroom. A small pile of books beneath the bedside table keeps favorite titles close at hand for nighttime reading. As a finishing touch, a single framed work is propped up on the far side of the bench.

CHAPTER ONE

HOME LIBRARIES

As long as there have been books, there have been book collectors—people who revel in the knowledge that the objects of their affection are close at hand, to be thumbed through, read, or merely gazed upon whenever the mood strikes. Like admirers of any precious item, book collectors easily become obsessed, buying one volume after another, even when the bookshelves in their homes are filled to capacity. This is no deterrent to such folk. Quite the contrary: A room brimming with books and little else is the aspiration of all avid book collectors. As former British prime minister William Gladstone observed more than a century ago, "If you go into a room and find it full of books—even without taking them from the shelves they seem to speak to you, to bid you welcome."

Rooms "full of books," or libraries, have graced the most fashionable homes for centuries and have enjoyed a comeback of sorts in recent years. The library as we know it today began to take shape during the latter half of the seventeenth century. Although books had been displayed alongside silver, porcelain, and other

OPPOSITE: Colors culled from nature pair well with the browns, reds, greens, and blacks of antique leather bindings. The muted pine-green chosen for the walls in this library is a case in point. Other earth tones that would pair well with a large collection like this include wheat, walnut, and a deep tomato-red similar to the one seen on the kilim-covered settee. The large scale of the bookshelves invites equally impressive artwork to be hung nearby; the two engravings in antique gold frames nicely fit the bill. Smaller prints parade above the top shelf, enlivening a plain wood panel. Precious porcelain, statuary, and other possessions break up wide rows of books and draw the eye upwards, further emphasizing the grand proportions of the room.

To accentuate the spacious proportions of the library in this Italian villa, the walls, rafters, and bookcases are painted white. Large spaces such as this can easily accommodate bold details like the sixteenth-century oak cathedral lectern in the foreground and the Emilio Pucci rug underfoot. Chicken-wire grilles and framed drawings adorn bookcase doors (detail, **OPPOSITE**). A less conventional furnishing is the bamboo sling chair from the nineteenth century, which offers an attractive yet equally comfortable alternative to the plush seating commonly found in libraries.

symbols of wealth in aristocratic dwellings prior to that time, it was then that a separate room devoted to their storage and study became de rigueur in a gentleman's home. Some of the most beautiful private libraries in history date to eighteenth century France and England, where leading architects of the day designed magnificent rooms, elegantly appointed with distinct areas for study and for socializing.

By the nineteenth century it was the rare home of style that lacked a library. Many of the house plans featured in Andrew Jackson Downing's *Victorian Cottage Residences* (first published in 1842 as *Cottage Residences*) assign libraries equal stature with the parlor, drawing room, and dining room in terms of square footage. "This hall is of ample size to serve as a dining room," Downing writes, "and this disposition would doubtless be preferred during at least part of the year, as it would allow the apartment on the left to be devoted entirely to a library."

The home library was still very much in vogue early in the 1900s, but as the century progressed, the room came to be viewed as a symbol of a bygone era—something that scholars still had need for, perhaps, but not the average citizen. Architects and interior designers eagerly reapportioned the newly found space for extra bedrooms, eat-in kitchens, family rooms, and the like. But the past decade has witnessed a shift in taste as more people have begun viewing the library not as an arcane notion but as an old-fashioned idea ripe for reinvention. More and more, spare rooms undergo conversion and new rooms are incorporated into blueprints. Savvy homeowners—especially those book collectors with overflowing shelves—have discovered that libraries are not only sophisticated additions to a house, they are also eminently sensible.

CREATE YOUR OWN LIBRARY

Anyone wishing to create a home library will first need to analyze the books that will occupy the space. Does the collection number in the thousands? If so, a spacious room with ample shelving will be required to accommodate it. More modest collections can be attractively housed in a stately bookcase or along a single wall of shelves. Are the books especially old and delicate? Glass doors in front of the shelves should certainly be considered to keep out dust, one of the main culprits behind book damage. Extremely rare books may even necessitate a climate-controlled environment. If any of the volumes are particularly decorative or historically significant, a prominent display area such as a bookstand or a small easel on a shelf might be desirable.

Next, identify the room in the house most suitable for the task at hand. If there is only one room available, you can immediately shift your concentration to decorating it. If more than one option exists, however, determine which

RIGHT: A wall of bookshelves turns the dressing area pictured here into a charming library. The deep rust-red complements the warm brown tones of the books from yesteryear. Note the single red shelf edge at eye level, a subtle design detail. A "doorway" cut out of the shelving is filled with a large mirror to visually expand the small space. A collection of favorite things including a portrait of the owner's great-grandfather rests on a small table. The step stool folds up when not in use.

OPPOSITE: Nowhere is it written that libraries must be decorated solely in staid colors and deep wood tones. Like all other rooms in the house, the library should reflect its owner's personal style. Dark gray-blue on the walls and bookshelves —Farrow & Ball's Down Pipe—creates a cozy yet sophisticated family room in this Los Angeles home. The color accentuates and draws the eye to the vibrant reds and yellows of the book covers.

interior meets more of the requirements of a library. Some questions to ponder include the following: Which room has the greatest amount of wall space away from direct sunlight, heaters, and air conditioners? Which is situated in a quieter part of the house? Which will afford you the most privacy when you want to read? People without an entire room to spare need not lose heart. Our modern vision of the home library includes many spaces that would have been unthinkable in the past—foyers, dressing areas, stair landings, and garden rooms, to name a few. Once outfitted with shelves and furnishings, these unexpected spots become havens every bit as inviting as their more traditional counterparts.

When transforming a 1907 water tank into a light-filled living space, an architect and an art professor positioned their extensive library—500 linear feet of books in all—in the center of the floor plan (**LEFT**). Bookcases enclose three sides of the 16- by 16-foot space formed by this home's four structural columns (**BELOW**). Black shelves echo the steel railings used elsewhere in the interior. The table designed by the owner to accommodate research projects and work conferences is fashioned from glass and steel, while the glass-and-steel bridge on the second level (**ABOVE**) allows natural light from the skylight to filter down to the first floor. After dark, the library is illuminated by small spotlights. Architectural models and other displays occupy the hard-to-reach center shelves up above.

Books arranged horizontally on this tall and narrow bookshelf counterbalance the elongated, vertical dimensions of the room. The neatly arranged stacks complement the elegance of the living room, while the spectrum of colorful spines serve as a cheerful addition to the subdued beige, green and white color scheme.

Shelves constitute the skeleton of a library, and as such should be settled upon before any other decorating decisions are made. Determining how much shelving you'll need to house your collection requires some calculation. For each linear foot of shelving, approximate eight to twelve average or medium-sized hardcover novels (or books of equivalent size) or six to eight large hardcovers (such as reference works, history tomes, and art monographs). To prevent sagging, no shelf should extend more than forty inches between supports. Once you know how much shelf space you will need, you may turn your attention to the kind of shelves you prefer. Built-in shelving is arguably the most classic look for a library, and designing such a unit allows a homeowner to include favorite elements, such as a floor-to-ceiling plan; storage cabinets along the lower portion of the room; recessed lighting; and niches for seating, artwork, or a writing surface. Freestanding bookcases, on the other hand, are more cost-effective and versatile, offering countless placement and style options. Once the shelving is in place, its outward appearance—a wood stain, for instance, or a coat of paint—is a personal choice that will depend greatly on the overall decoration of the room.

DECORATING THE LIBRARY

In their 1897 book, *The Decoration of Houses*, Edith Wharton and Ogden Codman Jr. set down the cardinal rule for decorating a library that still holds true to this day. "The general decoration of the library," they wrote, "should be of such character as to form a background or setting to the books, rather than to distract attention from them." Heed this advice, and nearly all decisions you make about wall colors, window treatments, and floor coverings can result in a pleasant environment. In most cases solid colors on the walls and understated patterns on fabric and carpeting are optimal, but even within these confines the possibilities for personal expression are endless. Putting your own stamp on your library's decor is important. As Wharton and Codman pointed out, "The individual tastes and habits of the people who are to occupy [a room] must be taken into account; it must not be 'a library,' but the library best suited to the master or mistress of the house."

Regarding furniture and accessories, the same decorating edict applies. Pieces may be traditional in appearance or ultramodern, as long as they do not detract attention from the books. A writing table and at least one comfortable reading chair are necessities in a library; other furnishings to consider if space allows are a small sofa or settee for social gatherings, a large work surface for research projects, and side tables on which to rest reading glasses or cups of tea. Typical library accessories include ladders to reach high shelves, book stands on which to display attractive volumes, and icons of curiosity and learning such as globes, maps, telescopes, and magnifying glasses. Artwork, collections, and family snapshots can be incorporated into the scheme but should be kept to a favorite few to maintain the focus on the books.

Anyone enamored with the look of a library but lacking a sufficient number of books can improvise in several ways. For example, cabinet doors can be covered with "faux book spines," while walls can be papered with a book motif. Boxes of old books with handsome bindings or dust jackets can often be purchased for a song at flea markets, rummage sales, and country auctions. There are even companies that sell old editions in bulk to decorators. Gently worn volumes have more character than brand-new ones, so cleaning out a bookstore is not recommended. As the pioneering interior designer Elsie de Wolfe commented in her 1913 style guide, *The House in Good Taste,* "You'd rather have [old books] with all their germs and dust than the soulless tomes of uncut pages. You can judge people pretty well by their books, and the wear and tear of them."

Trompe l'oeil wallpaper depicting rows of books creates the illusion of a library in this workspace. Auction catalogues stacked neatly on the desk mirror the bold red of the file cabinets down below and the "faux volumes" on the walls.

Recessed shelves and an all-white color scheme allow the books to take center stage in this elegant library. A generously sized Georgian desk with armchairs on either side can be used for solitary study or tête-à-têtes, while a larger seating area with a comfortable sofa, chairs, and cushioned stools is conducive to spirited discussions. The owner has devoted an entire shelf to the display of a single bowl (upper left) which draws attention to the cherished object. The graceful antique library steps add a sculptural element to the room.

{ A CLOSER LOOK }

IN A MANHATTAN LOFT, FLOOR-TO-CEILING MAPLE SHELVES BRING AN AIRY FEELING TO THE LIBRARY. A COORDINATING MAPLE LIBRARY LADDER PROVIDES EASY ACCESS TO UPPER SHELVES.

BRIGHTLY COLORED SLIDING PANELS COVER STORAGE AREAS AND ADD A HINT OF COLOR TO THE SPACE, WHILE OFF-WHITE STORAGE BOXES BLEND INTO THE BACKDROP OF THE ROOM SO AS NOT TO DETRACT ATTENTION FROM THE BOOKS.

THE SHELF EDGES EXTEND A FEW INCHES AROUND THE DOORWAY, CREATING DISPLAY AREAS FOR PRIZED POSSESSIONS.

OPPOSITE: In lofts and homes with open floor plans, carving out space for a library may require a creative eye. The owner of this Parisian apartment saw potential in the area below a staircase. Shelves are fully utilized but not overcrowded. The arrangement of the books themselves—standing upright, lying flat, leaning to one side—underscores the casual style of this interior.

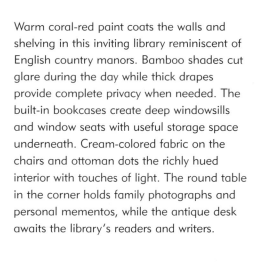

Warm coral-red paint coats the walls and shelving in this inviting library reminiscent of English country manors. Bamboo shades cut glare during the day while thick drapes provide complete privacy when needed. The built-in bookcases create deep windowsills and window seats with useful storage space underneath. Cream-colored fabric on the chairs and ottoman dots the richly hued interior with touches of light. The round table in the corner holds family photographs and personal mementos, while the antique desk awaits the library's readers and writers.

{ A CLOSER LOOK }

This elegant mahogany unit was discovered in London's Olympia antiques fair. Its glass doors prevent dust from settling on the books, an essential safeguard for rare books and antiquarian volumes.

Incorporating artwork and collections on the shelves breaks up the long lines of book spines and personalizes the interior.

The bookcase stands on a nine-inch black plinth to increase its height.

OPPOSITE: The pine paneling of these large, Georgian style built-in bookshelves add elegance and warmth to this Long Island, NY home's library. Bookshelves are a great place to showcase art—The Julia Condon mandala painting hung on this bookcase adds a contemporary touch and relaxes this traditional library's formality.

LEFT: In a Manhattan penthouse, a wall of bookshelves is temporarily topped with boxwood for the holidays. Painted pristine white, with whimsical lamps set at mid-height, these built-in shelves form the perfect backdrop to this engaging living room. The books, organized by category—including biographies, reference books, art books, and a collection of Modern Library editions—are interspersed with cherished objects to add visual interest to the scene.

OPPOSITE: An antique flip-top game table in this stylish Manhattan apartment's library is used as a dining table, allowing a couple to dine amidst their books and treasures. Interior designer Miles Redd designed the ebonized wood and sterling bookshelf, where a color block painting by Leora Armstrong is displayed. The shelves and walls of the room are lacquered in Farrow & Ball's Hague Blue, described by Redd as "a great way to do a moody color because of the way it reflects light. It doesn't look dark so much as rich. "

Above all else, a library should meet the needs of its owners. Here, matching work areas provide ample space for a couple's individual research projects and creative pursuits. The warm ocher walls, tiled floor, and towering bookcase conjure up images of Italian villas. Be sure to measure doorways and entryways before purchasing large furnishings like the desks and bookcase.

This library's décor reflects a garden writer's passion for her field. Custom-designed shelving has been painted black and marbleized, a dramatic effect against the grass-green walls.

Volumes with decorative covers face outward to give dimension to the orderly rows of books. Varied shelf height also adds to the layered, artistic look of this arrangement

The stack of book-shaped boxes forms a functional side table and brings a touch of whimsy to this otherwise studious space. Fresh flowers and floral-pattern chairs enliven the scholarly atmosphere of the library.

LEFT: Small paintings suspended over the bookshelves personalize one art lover's library. Hung with picture wire and art hooks, the canvases can be removed and replaced to search for a particular title, though it's probably best to keep oft-used books in plain sight. When designing custom shelving for small rooms, take advantage of every available space, including the often overlooked area above doorways and windows.

OPPOSITE: In homes where space is an issue, unexpected areas may harbor hidden library potential. Here, bookshelves line the walls of a moderate-size entryway. A figural carpet disguises the front door and moves open with it. When outfitting any small space, choose appropriately proportioned furnishings like a diminutive writing table and a chair that can be tucked neatly away when not in use. Continuing the same wallpaper and border treatment from an adjoining room helps the alcove appear to be part of a larger space.

CHAPTER TWO

ALL THROUGH THE HOUSE

AT THE START OF EACH NEW PROJECT, ALL DECORATORS FACE THE SAME challenge: How to marry their own unique vision with the individual tastes of their clients. As most have learned over the years, incorporating a client's books into an interior scheme is one of the quickest and best ways to personalize a space. And because books are so versatile, the same set of volumes can be arranged in dramatically different ways to complement any style of design, whether it's ultramodern, decidedly old-fashioned, or somewhere in between.

Before we begin a room-by-room analysis of which types of books work best in which settings, we must first learn to view books as three-dimensional objects whose colors, sizes, and textures will help determine their decorative potential. Examine your own bookshelves. You may never have fully appreciated the rainbow of color to be found there. Consider the aesthetic possibilities of grouping all the red books together, for example, or everything in the green family, from deepest hunter to palest chartreuse. Do the same for size and texture.

OPPOSITE: A whitewashed bookcase fades into the all-white backdrop of this living room, drawing attention to the books found on its shelves. Chicken-wire doors add a layer of texture to the scene and echo the look of the sisal rug and baskets atop the bookcase and beside the hearth. (Wire doors are also a good idea if fragile items are arranged among the books.)

ROOM BY ROOM

First impressions are important, and well-appointed foyers set the tone for a home's décor and hint at the furnishings and accessories to be found within. For bibliophiles, books are a natural choice here. Although there are exceptions, bookcases filled with an abundance of volumes tend not to be the best look for entryways. A better bet is a small, artful arrangement on a hall table, such as a selection of vintage novels supported by decorative bookends, perhaps, or a small stack of art books acting as a pedestal for a bowl, lamp, or piece of sculpture. If you'd like, rest books beneath the table on a small stool or on the floor to continue the theme down below. There are no limits on the subject matter appropriate for a foyer, but in this setting it is the outward appearance of books that takes precedence over the content.

Book collections that occupy the living room commonly represent the shared interests of the family. As such, they should be given pride of place. Begin by standing in the center of the room and surveying your surroundings. Is there an uninteresting wall that could benefit from built-in shelving? Or do you notice an unused area between two doorways that calls out for a stately bookcase? Maybe there are flat surfaces—a mantel, a desk, an ottoman, or a side table—where books could be placed to add visual interest to the scene. Once the display areas have been settled on, the books can be arranged in any number of ways such as meticulous rows, haphazard piles, or careful still lifes that incorporate precious possessions. The exact manner that will work best for you will depend on the overall style of the room; feel free to play with placement until you hit upon something you love.

Dining rooms may seem like unusual places to display books, but this is an attractive idea that more and more people have come to appreciate. There are three options that work especially well in this setting. The first is positioning a low cabinet with glass doors near the dining table so that the top can be used as a sideboard. The second is refitting a hutch for book storage. The third is installing a full wall of shelves. Because the dining table can be used for writing

ABOVE: Prominently placed in a foyer or just inside an exterior door, books announce this homeowner's passion for reading. A column of small stacks—on the tabletop, stool, and floor—form an eye-catching display. The bindings and dust jackets in white, gray, and dark green were chosen to quietly blend with the neutral setting.

OPPOSITE: The question of how to decorate stair landings has puzzled homeowners for years. Here is one good solution: Combine a handsome bookcase, a single armchair, a small table topped by cherished objects, and a series of framed engravings. The moss-green walls and upholstery fabric complement the antiquarian volumes on these shelves.

LEFT: The backdrop of books and artworks is an unconventional yet inspired idea for the dining room. Imagine the dinner-party discussions such a setting would spark. Art hooks attached to the front of the shelves make it easy to hang and rearrange frames. Glossy tomato-red paint and soft lights at the top of each column of shelves create a welcoming ambience.

BELOW: A commanding bookcase furnishes this elegant home office. The carefully selected books and objets d'art are especially pleasing to the eye when set against the same barn-red hue as the ceiling and draperies. To attain such harmonious arrangements in your own home, play with placement until each shelf is slightly different from the next. Here, some shelves are occupied entirely by books, some by collections, and others by a combination of both. To create a layering effect, hang a frame in front of the shelves.

ABOVE: Books can conform to any decorating style, whether pared down or over-the-top. In this lively living room, open shelves brimming with a haphazard arrangement of volumes blend well with the owner's copious and colorful collections.

OPPOSITE: The owners of this light-filled living room took to heart the words of Roman statesman Cicero: "A room without books is like a body without a soul." A plaque proclaiming these words rests on a dramatic mantel-top mountain of old volumes (top left). On the bookshelves, tomes of similar age and style bring the warm brown tones across the room, and alternating horizontal and vertical placement adds visual interest. A quartet of books on the coffee table creates a flat surface a bit higher than the table's. Arrangements like these are examples of the current trend to use books for decorative purposes.

ABOVE: In this small Nantucket bedroom a few shelves have been built into a custom-designed niche. This creative use of space puts everything within arm's reach of the bed—books occupy the top two shelves, while a handy reading light is located in the bottom nook.

LEFT: A creative use of paint can transform ordinary bookshelves (and the volumes they hold) into a vibrant part of a room's decoration. Here, wheat and lavender contrast well with the sunflower-yellow of the walls. The shelf above the window was reserved for a folk art display. On the coffee table, a stack of books elevates a small sculpture.

ABOVE: A room's color scheme can carry over to the bookshelves. In this airy summer cottage, paper book covers and brown leather bindings reflect the two-tone décor. (The paper covers also protect books from fingers covered with suntan lotion.) Shelf arrangements vary: Some hold all-white elements, some all-brown, and some a mixture of the two. One shelf in the middle houses a collection of white ceramics. Other objects stand between volumes or on top of them, like the wooden box and the graceful sculpture below it. Narrow shelves store magazines, while a long shelf up above supports a large collection of wooden candlesticks. Elsewhere in the room, short stacks of books elevate lamps on the desk and side table.

OPPOSITE: Paper covers can make a book collection coordinate with any décor. White book covers blend into the black-and-white color scheme that was chosen to visually expand the cozy interior of a seaside cottage. White ceramics, statuary, and other objects intermingle with the books, adding dimension to the scene.

BELOW: The stately cupboard-turned-bookcase pictured here dominates the potting shed. The arrangement of gardening books and favorite collections is simple to re-create. Each of the top shelves received a single large element, like the vintage picnic baskets that were used in this case. The next shelf down has stacks of equal size on the outer edges and similar objects—green McCoy mixing bowls—at the center. One shelf down the order is reversed: stacks of books stand in the center while green ceramics rest on the sides. The bottom shelf holds a decorative pitcher and shorter piles of frequently used volumes, each topped with a green plate.

ABOVE: In a small home office, these built-in bookcases take full advantage of high ceilings. Books are clustered into neat rows and stacks to underscore the clean lines of the space. Storing magazines in matching organizers helps avoid a cluttered look.

OPPOSITE: Cubby shelves on either side of a small window are a wonderful way to transform an out-of-the-way space. The lower inside cubby of each unit is left empty to display antiques. Matching side chairs, a drop-leaf table, and a single blue-and-white bowl complete the charming scene.

Books are essential accessories in a bedroom. Here, twin bookcases flank two sunny windows, which themselves flank a wonderfully sculptural bed, creating a noticeable sense of symmetry in the space. The long line of the drapes reinforces the height of the bookcases. Family photos and favorite possessions are interspersed with the books on shelves that are arranged in an open manner. No shelf is overstuffed; if filled to their limit, the bookcases might dominate the other furnishings in the room.

{ A CLOSER LOOK }

IN THIS SERENE BEDROOM,
BOOKS HAVE BEEN USED VERY
PRECISELY ON THESE SHELVES.
BOOKS WITH WHITE SPINES
REFLECT THE ABUNDANT USE OF
WHITE IN BEDDING, FURNISHINGS,
AND FLOOR COVERING.

THE SHELVES ARE ARRANGED
SPARSELY TO UNDERSCORE THE
SIMPLICITY OF THE OVERALL
DECORATING SCHEME,
AND TO ALLOW THE NEUTRAL
BACKGROUND OF THE
BOOKCASE TO STAND OUT.

SMALL WOODEN BOXES ARE SET
ATOP STACKS OF BOOKS WHILE
LARGER ONES STAND ALONE.
A SUBTLE ZIGZAG EFFECT IS
ACHIEVED BY ALTERNATING THE
PLACEMENT OF BOXES AND
PICTURE FRAMES ON EACH SHELF.
THE WHITE BOOKS, WOODEN
BOXES, AND BLACK-AND-WHITE
PHOTOGRAPHS HARMONIZE WITH
THE ROOM'S DÉCOR.

ABOVE: Books play an important supporting role in this sunken living room. They can be found throughout the space—on the coffee table, occupying modular bookcases around the sofa, and inside a curtained unit beside the window. The cotton poplin curtains shade the books from the sun and keep dust at bay. The owner has wisely placed some volumes on their side, an arrangement that catches the eye and reduces the stress on the bindings of large books. Positioning a banquette beneath a window that is flanked by bookcases created a welcoming window seat, one of the loveliest reading spots imaginable.

OPPOSITE: A book-filled étagère made of iron and wood anchors this eclectic living room. A full-length wall-to-wall mirror covers the wall behind the shelves, adding depth to the room. Bookshelf top space, often unemployed, is used here to showcase colorful artwork and decorative objects.

LEFT: No corner of the house is too humble to harbor a display of books. Here, the lower portion of the bookshelf is used for firewood; favorite volumes up above can be pulled down for quiet moments beside the woodstove.

OPPOSITE: In this romantic bedroom beneath the eaves, bookshelves have been built into the existing structure of the house. A collection of green-glazed ceramics creates a subtle pyramid beside the books; three vases on the bottom, then above them two, then one.

CHAPTER THREE

BOOKS AS DETAILS

"How obvious and valuable a means of decoration is lost by disregarding the outward appearance of books," opined Edith Wharton and Ogden Codman Jr. in *The Decoration of Houses*. When Wharton and Codman collaborated on their pioneering work in the waning days of Queen Victoria's reign, bookcases brimming with leather-bound volumes were a common sight in tasteful homes. Bookcases, it must be stated, were the only proper places for books. Rarely did a book rest on a side chair unless the person reading it had left it there unintentionally. Rarer still was the sight of successive stacks of books lined up on a coffee table or along a bench in a hallway. Over the course of the past century, such previously unorthodox scenarios have become commonplace, presenting decorators and creative homeowners with countless opportunities to use books as one uses a beautiful ceramic or fresh flowers—as a finishing touch that completes a room's décor.

Would scenes like those mentioned above have caused Wharton and Codman to raise an eyebrow? Quite possibly. But even they would have to concede that their plea for readers to appreciate the "outward appearance" of books may have sown the seeds of the current trend. For once you truly examine the outward appearance of the books you

OPPOSITE: Piled into colorful towers on the coffee table, a book collection becomes the focal point of this living room in neutral tones. Special attention was given to the placement of color: Notice how the bold red spines have been distributed, coaxing the eye to move from one stack to the next.

own, the more obvious their decorative potential becomes. Books can add a burst of color to a neutral space, contribute texture to a tabletop still life, and create a flat surface suitable for a vase, a bowl, or a wine glass. They can draw the eye toward an elegant mantel or divert attention from a viewless window. The subtlety or strength of their presence in your home is a matter of personal preference; the range of options regarding their placement can be as limitless as your imagination.

DECORATIVE ARRANGEMENTS

There are three basic ways that books can be arranged aside from their traditional bookshelf perch: in stacks, in rows, and as single volumes. Stacks can be short, only two to three books high, or as tall as you please as long as there is no risk of

Mantels are natural focal points in a room, and as such are often used for artistic displays. Books can be incorporated into any arrangement; the number and appearance of books will depend greatly on the style of the room. In this classically appointed living room, a simple stack of books stands opposite a trio of art glass. The gold and brown hues of the book jackets complement the decorative mirror up above. Setting a single object on top of the books has made a nice finishing touch.

toppling. They can be placed on any number of surfaces including the floor, where substantial stacks can act as side tables, telephone tables, and even pedestals for pieces of sculpture. When building a stack, pay attention to its overall appearance. Perfectly aligned piles complement modern or pared-down interiors, while those that are slightly askew fit well in less defined settings. Color is another important

In an art lover's home office, a stack of books acts as a pedestal for a piece of sculpture. Care was taken to create a tower that tapers slightly toward the top. Colors, too, were carefully arranged: Black, white, red, orange, and yellow spines are evenly distributed so that no single hue is dominant.

ABOVE: Baskets hold unlimited potential for book storage. In this living room, volumes are artfully arranged in a basket. The basket is set beside a nonworking fireplace; if it were a working hearth, fireside placement would not only create a safety hazard, it would quickly desiccate the bindings and the paper.

OPPOSITE: Placed on a table, dresser, or sideboard, bookstands can be the centerpieces of attractive displays. Choose a favorite volume and turn to an appealing image. To re-create the pared-down arrangement shown here, position matching lamps on either side of the table and a single sculptural object beside the bookstand.

consideration: Spread bold hues evenly throughout a stack (or series of stacks) by interspersing spines in neutral tones or softer shades. Once every few months, rotate volumes within very tall stacks to prevent placing stress on the bindings.

Like stacks, rows of books can be short or long, meticulously ordered or casually grouped. They can be made up of individual volumes that all relate to one subject (photography, perhaps, or gardening) or be part of a set, such as encyclopedias or a collection of Hardy Boys mysteries (the latter providing a wonderful band of blue in a room). Rows can occupy nearly any surface in your home and be arranged either side by side or front to back, leaning backward slightly to reveal the tops of each book. Rows can also be composed of a series of single volumes lined up along the back of a sideboard or on a wide wainscoting. Books that face into a room in this manner should be of an artistic nature—exhibiting lovely gold-leaf decoration, a vintage dust jacket, or eye-catching graphics, for example—and should be positioned away from direct sunlight.

A single book can be displayed on its own or incorporated into a tabletop still life. A volume that stands alone should be large or graphically intriguing to warrant the special attention. Books can be laid flat on a surface with the covers closed (if the cover art is especially pleasing) or opened to a particular page to reveal a favorite illustration or portion of text. To highlight text, set a decorative magnifying glass directly on top of the passage. Bookstands are also a useful accessory in such arrangements, emphasizing your choice to showcase a particular book. When including a book in a tabletop still life, keep in mind that the items chosen for such displays should be visually interesting by themselves and complement one another when combined. Therefore, a vintage volume with a well-worn cover will look best with antique or rustic objects; a book with a more modern appearance will pair well with contemporary forms.

There are few limits on the type of surfaces appropriate for displays of stacks, rows, and single volumes as long as the condition of the books is not threatened by a close proximity to heaters, air conditioners, or windows that are

LEFT: Although the area beneath a table generally goes unnoticed, this hallway display shows why we should all take a second look. A trio of books in sherbet shades adds visual interest to the arrangement here. The style of table will determine the number and size of volumes that will work best. For example, the graceful lines of this table are easily overpowered, so three thin volumes was just the right touch. A chunkier table could have supported a taller stack or a trio of thicker books.

OPPOSITE: The single side chair pictured here supports a hallway still life. On top, the trio of books provides a flat surface for a sculptural horn and a bold yellow vase. Even in groupings as small as three, the colors of book spines are thoughtfully arranged: The darkest spine anchors the display while the red, set directly beneath the vase, adds an extra dash of color to the neutral scene.

frequently left open. Books displayed on or near a mantel should be moved when the fireplace is in use. Tables are among the most common choices for an arrangement of books. Any kind of table can be utilized, including desks, dining tables, bedside tables, and coffee tables. The tops of dressers, vanities, chests, and short cupboards are also ideal. Chairs, too, offer some good possibilities for placement. For obvious reasons, a chair chosen for an artful display should not be one that is used frequently; chairs that stand in a hallway or flank a sideboard are better bets. Look around a room to find additional ideas: Is there a mantel, wall niche, or wide molding around the top of the room? Essentially, any flat surface in your home can be considered.

A whole other realm of possibilities opens up to anyone who can spot decorative potential in unusual objects and accessories. With a creative touch and perhaps a little

RIGHT: Set on a small table, a stack of books becomes a stylish telephone stand. Confining the book colors to white, black, red, and gray gives the arrangement a cohesive feeling and complements the room's modern décor.

OPPOSITE: This nineteenth-century circus ladder, formerly used to mount elephants, now serves as an unusual and attractive perch for books. Volumes with personal significance to the owner can be displayed with their covers in full view while others can be chosen purely for their colors. The red, blue, and lavender bands shown here complement the overall color scheme of the room.

dusting, ladders, garden benches, baskets, vintage luggage, architectural salvage, and even an antique Flexible Flyer sled can all support attractive book displays. Look for such items at antiques malls, flea markets, and yard sales. When examining a piece, ask yourself whether it could support a book on its top, on an edge, or inside. Keep an eye out for books while on these treasure hunts; volumes with old leather covers, eye-catching graphics, and subtly faded colors are commonly found at the same venues. Artfully aged books can also be unearthed at used bookstores; check the sale racks and one-dollar boxes for books that are too damaged for collectors but are ideal for still lifes. Artistic types have been known to spin such castoffs into decorative gold.

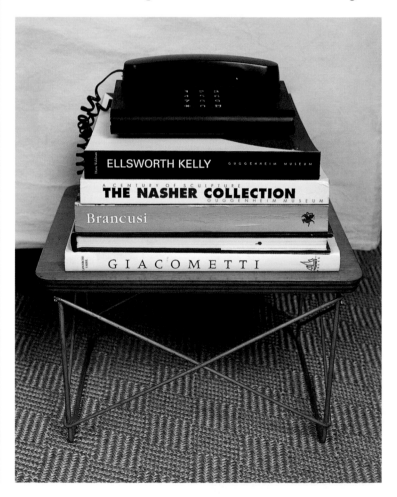

Provence Interiors

Books are placed throughout this spacious
living room that calls to mind the stately
country homes of Europe. On a large
round table, stacks encircle a grand floral
arrangement. Such displays offer the residents
endless opportunity to rearrange volumes and
reposition favorite objects atop the literary
perches. The groupings also encourage
guests to meander through room, consider
the titles, retire to the comfortable sofa,
and lose themselves in a book.

{ A CLOSER LOOK }

THE DESIGN BOOKS DISPLAYED THROUGH-
OUT THIS BRIGHT LIVING ROOM ADD TO
THE GLAMOUR OF THE SPACE. SOME
VOLUMES SUPPORT VASES AND OTHER
OBJECTS, WHILE OTHERS SIMPLY INVITE
GUESTS TO PICK THEM UP. A TRIO OF
BOOKS RAISES A DELICATE CRYSTAL
CANDELABRA IN A TABLETOP SCHEME.

BOOKS CREATE A FLAT SURFACE ON A
CUSHIONED BENCH AND PROVIDE THE
PERFECT RESTING SPOT FOR A COLORFUL
FLORAL ARRANGEMENT.

ON A LARGE OTTOMAN, FOUR EQUAL
STACKS CENTERED AROUND A GAZING BALL
FORM A DRAMATIC FOCAL POINT FOR
THE ROOM.

OPPOSITE: A prominent, well-lit table is a wonderful place for book
displays. Here, stacks vary in height and each is topped by an object or
collection. Another stack, also with an object atop it, rests on an armchair
nearby. Don't be afraid to add a touch of whimsy to a scene; note that
the copy of the children's classic *Eloise* (in the pile beneath the wooden
box) shares space with books for grown-ups on art, fashion, and design.

LEFT: Cozy corners can be difficult to decorate; books provide a simple and stylish solution. The stacks are set on a low table nestled between an armchair and a striped futon. The sunny window provides ample light for reading. When not plucked from the pile by readers, the books support a pair of potted ivy plants and a decorative bowl.

BELOW: A child's chair holds a stack of books beside the tub. Other possibilities on a similar scale include a footrest and a hatbox.

OPPOSITE: The low wooden bench, matching slip-covered side chairs, and an imposing antique portrait set the stage for this dramatic hallway display. Stacks of books that alternate high and low are lined up on the bench. The outer stacks support charming topiaries; other piles are topped with cherished objects. The supporting role of the volumes in the overall arrangement is underscored by the fact that the spines do not face outward; hence, no titles may be discerned. The page edges create strong white bands that echo the stripes of the wallpaper.

BELOW: Using books as a pedestal in tabletop still lifes is a trick of the decorator's trade. When arranging similar groupings in your own home, choose books that complement the other objects on the table. For instance, volumes with warm tones and considerable wear look great when paired with antiques (*Picturesque America*, Volumes I and II are shown here). Sleek, glossy design books will likely look better alongside contemporary art and sculpture.

ABOVE: Short stacks of books chosen for their muted colors and art themes support a pair of cast-iron elements in this highly symmetrical scene. To set it up, a long table was placed beneath a quartet of prints. A single framed piece was then put in place to anchor the arrangement. Using the frame as a central point, two lamps, two plants, and the two stacks of books were positioned on either side. A rose bouquet in a pretty silver pot offers the perfect finishing touch.

OPPOSITE: When chosen by color, books can reinforce a room's décor. Here, black-and-white art books share shelf space with a collection of black-and-white photographs in a room dominated by white walls and a black mantel.

BOOKS FIGURE PROMINENTLY
IN THIS ELEGANT ARRANGE-
MENT THAT CAN EASILY BE
RE-CREATED IN ANY HALLWAY
OR LIVING ROOM.

THE MATCHING LAMPS AND
SIDE CHAIRS ADD A SENSE OF
SYMMETRY TO THE SCENE.

SHORT STACKS OF BOOKS CAN
BE TOPPED WITH FLOWER
VASES, PIECES OF SCULPTURE,
AND CHERISHED COLLECTIONS.
RESTING ANOTHER PILE OF
BOOKS ON A DECORATIVE
FOOTSTOOL UNDER THE TABLE
REINFORCES THE THEME
UP ABOVE.

OPPOSITE: A grouping of aging books becomes an integral part of this tabletop still life. Old books with a similar look can be found at antiques shops, flea markets, and used bookstores. Their condition need not be perfect; as you can see, some wear and tear complements the textures and colors of the other objects. When used purely as decorative details, the books can even be in a foreign language.

{ BOOKS AS DETAILS }

In this serene bedroom, the brightest splashes
of color are found in the curtains and the two
books resting on the narrow writing table. The
books' dust jackets were removed to reveal
the bold hues and matte finishes underneath.
Additional volumes—some wearing white
paper book covers to unify the group—occupy
a hand-carved mahogany pagoda.

RIGHT: In this living room, an architectural detail attached to the wall is an ideal resting place for books. A similar piece could be installed anywhere in the house to hold cookbooks in the kitchen, novels beside a bed, or beautiful fancy volumes In the foyer. Additional books occupy the top and bottom of a round side table, where they act as both decorative elements in the room and sources of good reading within easy reach of the chair.

OPPOSITE: The book lover in this home commissioned a specially designed headboard that incorporates a shelf for books. Small, neat stacks lined up in a row reflect the strong lines of the room and prevent a messy look. Beside the bed, larger volumes support a telephone and a colorful bouquet.

CHAPTER FOUR

BOOKSHELVES AS ARCHITECTURE

HERETOFORE WE HAVE SEEN NUMEROUS WAYS BOOKS MAY BE USED TO decorate a home. In most cases, it is the books that capture our attention; the shelves, tabletops, and mantels they occupy blend into the background of the room. This is as it should be, many bibliophiles believe. For others, however, the bookcase is as vital to a room's décor as the volumes that fill it. The latter group seeks out designs that function, even when empty, as interesting architectural elements. Once lined with books, these pieces pack even more of a visual punch. Often it is an architect who opts for this mode of display—someone who relishes the opportunity to manipulate a bookcase's inherently graphic grid pattern to create a one-of-a-kind design. Some people simply fall in love with an unusual form they see at a flea market or furniture showroom and buy it then and there.

If this approach appeals to you, here's how to find the best design for your home. First consider whether you prefer something custom-built or store-bought. Both have their positive attributes. Custom-built bookcases and

OPPOSITE: Sculptural structures can double as stylish bookcases. Here, wooden étagères (a second one is just visible in the foreground, and a third in the background) echo the shape of the colorful obelisks on the table and complement the room's eclectic décor. Stacks of books with spines facing outward fill each level and provide easy access to specific titles.

RIGHT: Bookcases with unusual shapes can stand alone as sculptural elements in a room. Filled with books, they take on an even grander air. This tapering model fits perfectly into a living room alcove, making it especially well suited to the space. Look for out-of-the-ordinary examples like this one in contemporary furniture stores or consult a carpenter or furniture designer about options for building a custom piece.

OPPOSITE: One of the joys of custom shelving is that you can incorporate any architectural style into its design. Neoclassical details including columns and a pediment distinguish the bookcases that frame the doorway in this master bedroom. A warm ecru paint offers a subtle contrast to the off-white of the wall's upper molding. Antique blue-and-white ceramic jars punctuate each corner of the unit. To find inspiration for your own home, peruse books on architecture—ancient, modern, and everything in between.

bookshelves allow a book collector to achieve the exact look he has in mind for the exact space that needs to be filled. They can be constructed of any material, finished in any paint color or wood stain, and trimmed with any number of decorative embellishments. Budget and time constraints can be an issue, though, since all but the simplest built-in designs cost more and take longer to install than freestanding bookcases purchased at furniture stores, antiques malls, or similar venues. There are many attractive store-bought models on the market today, but it may take some research to find the precise kind you like. Once you've selected something, it can be put in position as soon as it is delivered.

LEFT: As this room attests, the wall surrounding a window is an ideal spot to install custom shelving. Deep shelves that are arranged sparsely form an attractive grid pattern that enhances any space. Shelves can be painted to blend in with the wall color (like the creamy-white shade seen here), or they can wear a bolder hue. Painting only the back wall within each shelf is another option that adds depth and contrast when books and collections are set in front of it.

OPPOSITE: In this small apartment, plywood and brushed-aluminum bookshelves reach several feet above a doorway, making the most of the tall ceilings. The shelving's design complements the owner's large collection of mid-twentieth-century modern furniture and accessories. Collections can often inspire our choices of color and furnishings; analyze the objects in your possession to see if any spark ideas for bookcase designs in your own home.

LOCATION

The specific area in which you intend to display your books may inspire the style of bookshelves you choose. Bare walls, alcoves, doorways, and mantels are all focal points that invite innovative ideas. A large expanse of wall space, for example, can be handled in a number of ways. You might line the wall with shelves from floor to ceiling; to make this option especially striking, incorporate architectural details like columns or unusual materials like chrome, plywood, or plastic. Plans that surround a doorway or window garner additional interest. You might also install a wall unit that comprises shelves and cabinetry—unusual configurations or striking colors can personalize these designs.

Wall units can be as detailed or as plain as you like. In this living room, six large open shelves (one filled with a television) underscore the simplicity of the surroundings. Books are concentrated on the upper right and lower left shelves, encouraging the eye to move between the two. Framed photographs and favorite objects occupy the other shelves. Notice the short stack of books on the coffee table: Displaying several copies of the same book creates an artwork of sorts, in the spirit of Andy Warhol's soup cans.

Doorways are natural focal points in a room, so placing bookcases on either side is a simple way to achieve a striking effect. The tall designs seen here are well suited to a room with vaulted ceilings; the dark color of the bookcases makes them stand out in the whitewashed space.

Alcoves and niches, whether large or small, can also be fitted for attractive book storage. You can outfit such spaces with shelves or slide a freestanding bookcase into place. When installing shelves, consider using an exaggerated thickness of wood, a bold paint color, or a contrasting material like mahogany shelves set into a white wall niche. Anyone searching for a bookcase to fit a specific spot should carry not only the dimensions of the alcove but also the dimensions of the doorways leading into the room and into the house. Nothing is more disappointing than bringing home a piece of furniture only to find that it can't make it to its final destination.

Framing a doorway or mantel with similar elements like a pair of side chairs or two ornate cast-iron urns is a simple way to bring a sense of symmetry to a room. Bookcases are a natural choice to achieve the look. To make a bold statement, choose oversized or particularly creative designs. An unusual bookcase that stands out on its own looks even better when set opposite a mirror image of itself. And when positioned in this manner, tall models are transformed into architectural columns. Bookcase columns can be built-in or freestanding; wall anchors may be necessary if freestanding models are not entirely stable. Even a pair of run-of-the-mill bookcases can

A double-height bookcase becomes the focal point of this small house. The towering structure forms a partial stairwell. The reference books and volumes that are used frequently are stored on the lower shelves and in bookcases along the opposite wall (visible on the left). The upper shelves are accessed by a ladder stored out of sight.

OPPOSITE: In this living room with soaring ceilings, an alcove beside the fireplace was painted black to accentuate the height of the space. The choice of color also echoes the hues of the marble fireplace surround and the lacquered floor. Shelves built into the concave column support *objets trouvés* and books that were carefully selected to reflect the colors found elsewhere in the room: ocher, red, blue, and black.

ABOVE: In settings where color and pattern are high intensity, bookcases must possess a strong presence to hold their own. Matching wood-and-metal models by Italian designer Andrea Branzi stand their ground in the living room of this Hamptons hideaway; traditional bookcases would simply get lost in the mix. A large number of books are also displayed on the coffee table, underlining the fact that the shelving units were chosen as much for their look as for their storage capacity.

Set against navy-blue walls, the whitewashed cubby shelves pictured here take on the appearance of shadow boxes. The large size of the squares contributes to the artistic feeling. Units measuring three cubbies wide and four high occupy two walls of the space; on a third wall, a smaller three-by-two design hangs above a single long shelf (**OPPOSITE**). Books and collections are arranged with care; cluttered shelves would detract from the room's pared-down aesthetic.

flank a doorway or mantel to artistic effect; make them command attention by coating them with a vibrant paint color like fire-engine red or midnight blue. The books on the shelves can provide bursts of color as well. Choosing all spines in a single hue will underscore the symmetry of the scene, while bands of color—all green on one shelf, all black on the next, and so on—will energize the room.

ARCHITECTURE AND COLOR

Sometimes a room's distinguishing characteristics can inspire a bookcase's form or placement as well. Vaulted ceilings may call out for a towering design to complement the space and hold an entire family's collection of books. The upper shelves of tall designs can be reached by a library ladder, which in itself can become a sculptural element in a room. The open layout of a spacious loft may benefit from the creation of a semiprivate reading area; install cubby shelves extending out from a wall near a sunny corner. Cubbies that are open on both sides will allow light and air to filter through. And in attics where access is limited under the eaves, custom shelving can make use of those areas; unusual building materials like salvaged beams or metal piping can add visual interest.

The use of color to enhance and personalize a bookcase's appearance has been touched on in previous paragraphs, but should be emphasized again. Imagine the aesthetic possibilities of painting the same design in various ways: tangerine shelves against white walls, Prussian blue against warm rust-red, or white shelves against navy blue. In combination with decorative embellishments, paint can be doubly effective. Unifying a series of ordinary bookcases with a single color and an elegant crown molding, for instance, can bestow upon the units the look of custom designs. (To make them truly unique, choose a molding that is of a larger scale and a hue that stands out in the space.) Focusing a creative eye on what you already have in your home may yield architecturally intriguing ideas you hadn't noticed before.

Positioning narrow bookcases in spaces that are wide enough to accommodate larger pieces draws attention to the height and form of the designs you have chosen. Before being placed in this yellow setting, the twins units were painted white to match the room's woodwork and trim, reinforcing the architectural effect.

{ A CLOSER LOOK }

IN THIS CHIC COTTAGE, THE HOMEOWNER CHOSE TO FILL THE SHELVES EXCLUSIVELY WITH A COHESIVE COLLECTION OF BROWN LEATHER BOOKS THAT COMPLEMENTS THE ROOM'S RUSTIC STYLE.

THE SHELVES EXTEND UP TO THE SLOPING CEILING. THE ANGLED DESIGN EMPHASIZES THE DRAMATIC LINES OF THE ROOM.

PAINTING THE SHELVES GREEN AND THE BACK WALL BLUE MAKES THE BOOKS REALLY STAND OUT IN THE SPACE. SPOTLIGHTS ILLUMINATE THE BOOKSHELVES FROM THE RAFTERS.

OPPOSITE: Bookshelves transform the triangular wall space of this Swedish loft into a kaleidoscope of color. The shelves were painted white to blend into the background, allowing the books to take center stage. In the center, just below eye level, a whole shelf has been left bare for family photographs; vacation mementos are scattered throughout.

LEFT: Tall bookcases form columns of color in this serene setting. Embellished with gold leaf, the leather bindings form a cohesive pattern that complements the room's elegant furnishings. Family photographs and a peacock print break up the display of books and offer the eye a place to rest.

BELOW: Recessed spaces throughout the house can be transformed into book storage. Extra-wide shelves create a dramatic look in this art lover's home. Lined with books, the three narrow shelves up above contribute broad bands of color to the all-white room, and spotlights installed on the ceiling illuminate the volumes. One shelf divides the space below the books; a potted plant and two mirrors with ornate gilded frames stand on the shelf while a black leather ottoman resides underneath.

ABOVE: Back-painted, minimalist bookshelves create depth and highlight the bookcase's grid which echoes the linear, geometric design theme of this living room. Books arranged both vertically and horizontally recall the right angles of the shelves and the rest of the room.

OPPOSITE: A bold purple hue coats walls and woodwork in this family room. The wall unit features ample shelf space for books, family photographs, and precious possessions. The double shelf on the bottom accommodates a television; the cabinets below store movies out of sight. Alphabet blocks rest atop children's books on the top shelf. Combining books and collections that relate to one another is an inspiring idea—imagine old cameras with photography books, house models beside architecture books, seashells beside travel books, and so on.

Cubbies of varying sizes and shapes reach to the ceiling in this guest bathroom. The forest-green paint on the shelves picks up the darkest hue found in the bold palm-leaf wallpaper pattern. Books, collections, framed prints, and mirrors are loosely arranged on the shelves, contrasting with the stark look of the room.

{ A CLOSER LOOK }

In this architect's seaside home in California, books and collections share custom-designed shelving. Lights installed above the top shelf bathe the books and art collection in a soft glow when evening falls.

The top row is dedicated to folk art collectibles. The shelves and narrow niches accommodate large and small collections.

The height of the shelves is tall in order to accommodate the owner's collection of oversized books.

RIGHT: Shelves that extend far beyond arm's reach create a dramatic backdrop for a room. A case in point are the towering bookcases that flank the fireplace in this living room. With few exceptions, the shelves are filled with books from end to end, creating a tapestry effect of texture and hue. Library ladders are essential accessories for reaching upper shelves; a ladder rail runs the perimeter of the shelves and crosses over the mantel.

OPPOSITE: Wall niches support book collections in style, as these graceful arches fitted with wooden shelves attest. In this arrangement, the heights of the books vary from shelf to shelf, reflecting the casual feeling of the interior. On the round table draped with lovely linens, four stacks of art books surround a galvanized tin bucket brimming with hydrangea.

CHAPTER FIVE

BOOKNOTES

The question of where to begin a decorating project—especially when it involves displaying a collection—is always daunting. When it comes to arranging books, the number of options can seem overwhelming. To simplify the process and get you started in the right direction, we offer the following tips to cover the basics of book display in the home.

DETERMINE HOW MUCH SHELVING YOU'LL NEED

The amount of shelving required will depend not only on the size of your collection but also on the *stage* of your collecting. A person who has gathered thousands of books over a lifetime and has no plans to buy many more won't need to leave as much room for future acquisitions as someone just starting out.

Use this calculation to determine how much shelving you'll need:

• For each linear foot of shelving, approximate eight to twelve average or medium-sized hardcover novels (or books of equivalent size) or six to eight large hardcovers (such as reference works, history tomes, and art monographs). Adjust the numbers slightly for especially thin or thick volumes.

• To prevent sagging, no shelf should extend more than 40 inches between supports.

OPPOSITE: Sizable book collections need ample shelf space; packing volumes too tightly can weaken the spines. In this home library, built-in bookcases provide plenty of storage. The owner's interest in gardening is evident in the large selection of garden books, fruit-and-floral slipcovers, and framed bird prints on the wall.

A trio of freestanding bookcases assumes the look of a built-in design for a fraction of the cost. While most of the volumes stand vertically, a few are stacked on their sides, adding visual interest to the arrangement. Beside the sofa, a selection of large art books set atop a terra-cotta pedestal supports a small bronze animal.

DECIDE WHAT STYLE OF SHELVING IS RIGHT FOR YOU

Shelving can be constructed of any wood, from lightest ash to deepest mahogany. A coat of paint can make a bookcase coordinate with a room's existing woodwork—or stand out when set against it. To determine the best look for a particular setting, consider the overall decoration of the room as well as the architectural style of the house. Visit furniture showrooms with a digital camera or consult decorating magazines, tagging pictures that inspire you.

- Built-in bookcases have a classic look
- Freestanding designs are wonderfully versatile
- Angular cubby shelves work especially well in modern interiors
- Stately antique secretaries call to mind Old World estates
- Metal shelves lend themselves to a modern interior

BELOW: Designing built-in bookcases allows a homeowner to envision any configuration he likes. Here, a large space has been left empty to accommodate a settee and a framed antique screen. The backs of the bookshelves have been painted red to pick up the warm tones used elsewhere in the room.

ABOVE: A single bookcase, even loosely arranged, can enliven any space; this bookcase is of a stately design with wide crown molding situated in a living room alcove. A folding panel concealing an entertainment center is designed to look like two shelves of books. A painting hung in the middle of the shelves adds dimension to the scene. Three old volumes form a loose pyramid on top of the bookcase.

RIGHT: Filling an empty wall with bookshelves is a practical use of space. It is especially fitting for this structure—a former gardening shed reborn as guest quarters. The library ladder allows access to upper shelves and the sleeping loft up above.

OPPOSITE: Take advantage of existing alcoves throughout the house that can be transformed into handsome book storage. In this living room, recessed space beside the fireplace was fitted with bookshelves. Neat rows of old volumes form bands of color in the room. Two shelves, one slightly higher than the other, were reserved for cherished objects and vintage photographs.

THE BEST PLACES FOR BOOKCASES

Stand in the center of a room and look around you. Is there a space that seems like a natural choice for a bookcase or built-in shelving? There may be an existing niche beside a fireplace, an underutilized corner, or an empty space between two doorways. Long expanses of wall are ideal spots for built-in bookcases or a series of freestanding designs. Nearly any placement can be considered as long as the books will not reside in close proximity to a heater or air conditioner, or in direct sunlight.

In this serene living room, books are displayed in many inventive ways. One lies open on a decorative box (left, third shelf from bottom). Right below this (second shelf from the bottom), three volumes with gold-leaf decoration are flanked by a pair of books bearing a hint of orange; the whole grouping rests on top of two large books with gold-leaf pages facing outward.

HOW TO ARRANGE A SHELF

The manner in which books are displayed on a shelf depends on the personal taste of the homeowner and the overall look of a room. People with more modern sensibilities often admire uninterrupted rows or a series of stacks interspersed with the occasional sculptural object. Others prefer an eclectic mix of books, family snapshots, and collections. Play with placement: Break up a long row with a framed photograph or a lovely vase, rest a favorite possession on a short stack of books, or group volumes by color. Any arrangement that pleases your eye is acceptable as long as your ability to retrieve a particular title when you need it is not compromised.

Neat rows of books—and little else—line the shelves of an ebonized Napoleon III bibliothèque. Such arrangements bespeak simple elegance in a room. On the top shelf, stacks of books flank an antique mask, offering a counterpoint to the strong horizontal bands down below.

RIGHT: Here, a custom-designed bookcase features special display cases for artwork—in this case botanical prints in matching white frames. Above and below, books are arranged in uninterrupted rows. A single side chair underscores the room's modern look.

OPPOSITE: When it comes to arranging a shelf, some people believe that less is more; others love to combine books and artwork in an energetic mix. In this library, a lifetime's collection of books, prints, and photographs are layered to artistic effect. Especially decorative covers face outward to gain full appreciation.

INCORPORATING ARTWORK

There are many ways that small sculptures and framed works of art—paintings, prints, and photographs—can be combined with books. Small-scale works can fill gaps between books (the volumes form a natural frame around the piece). You might also leave an entire shelf empty for display; for tall items, the space may need to be two or three shelves high. Sculptures can also parade along the top of a bookshelf, while framed pieces can hang directly in front of the shelves. Although the frames will overlap some of the book spines in the latter scenario, works of art that are hung with picture wire can be easily lifted off when a particular title is needed.

Victorian books feature a wide range of colors and ornate decoration, making them not only fun to collect but attractive to display in the home. These stories for young readers were published late in the 1800s. Similar examples can often be found at flea markets, antiques malls, and used bookstores.

BOOK COLLECTING 101

Many people will gather hundreds of books over the span of a lifetime; collectors do not simply acquire books here and there but actively seek out new additions to their library. Whether their passion is modern first editions, a particular author, or a specific subject, such as children's books or cinematography, they are fully committed to finding as many examples as they can. Guidebooks on book collecting are good resources for anyone just starting out. To locate rare or out-of-print books, one should attend book fairs, frequent used-book dealers, scour garage sales, and surf the Internet. And never be afraid to ask questions of dealers or fellow collectors to help you become an expert in your area of interest.

CARING FOR YOUR BOOKS

Dust, sunlight, and moisture are major culprits of book damage in the home. Glass-fronted bookshelves are the best deterrent for dust and are recommended for rare volumes. Books resting on open shelves should be dusted regularly; run a vacuum on a low setting and with a soft brush attachment over the books. To prevent fading, keep books out of direct sunlight. Never pack books too tightly on a shelf, and always display them far from heaters and air conditioners. You may want to protect delicate volumes with Mylar book covers, available through art-supply stores. Finally, if such services are needed, inquire at a local museum or historical society for names of bookbinders and conservators near you.

An English regency bookcase also serves as a sideboard and entertainment center in this dining room. The symmetry of the carefully arranged books in the shelves surrounding the TV screen and the two plants placed on either side of the bookcase top help balance and integrate the TV—an otherwise out of place object—as a more natural object in the dining room.

ORGANIZING YOUR BOOKS

Different people have different ways of organizing their books. Some sort by author, some by subject, and some by size. Any method is acceptable as long as it makes sense to you and you can find a particular title without having to conduct an extensive search. Novels might be arranged according to the time in your life when you read them (grammar school, high school, or college), alphabetically by author, or by the period in history when they were written. Generally it is a good idea to divide large collections into sub-categories (art, travel, literature), and then divide the sub-categories into smaller categories (art by artists, travel by destination) or organize them alphabetically by author.

LEFT: Yet another contemporary take on the reading nook features a black leather wing chair set against a backdrop of black walls and draperies. The perfectly poised reading lamp completes the scene.

OPPOSITE: Not only can book collections be sorted by subject within a single bookcase, they can also be broken down and displayed in separate rooms: cookbooks in the kitchen, art books in the living room, travel books in the den, and so on. In this bedroom novels, merely a portion of a larger book collection, occupy most of the built-in bookshelves.

RIGHT: Positioned beside a window, the comfortable armchair and ottoman of one lifelong reader create a welcoming reading nook. Antiquarian volumes stand behind the glass doors of his secretary; literature, gardening, and design are just a few of the subjects to be found in the elegant wheeled shelves that stands within arm's reach of the chair.

BELOW: The handsome pair of bookends displayed here supports antiquarian volumes with decorative gold-leaf designs. Bookends are highly collectible and can be found in a variety of materials: marble, wood, and cast iron, to name a few. Single pieces that are missing their mate can be used to support one end of a row of books while the other end abuts the side of a bookcase or a wall.

OPPOSITE: Library ladders are a wonderful example of form following function. Allowing access to books set on high shelves makes these objects useful; styles that complement nearly every décor make them welcome additions in any room. The texture of this studded model enhances the matte black paint of the bookshelves.

CREATING A READING NOOK

There are two elements that are essential for an inviting reading nook—a comfortable chair and a good source of light. While a bright window is ideal for daytime reading, a lamp should also stand at the ready for evenings and overcast days. Additional details enhance the comfort factor of the space. Ottomans and footrests, for example, encourage relaxation. A small side table is another useful piece, perfect for holding a stack of books and a cup of tea. If there is more than one place in your home to situate a reading nook, choose the quietest part of the house and the room with the least foot traffic; a garden view is especially calming.

LADDERS, BOOKSTANDS, AND OTHER FINISHING TOUCHES

Over the years, items that were once purely functional have come to be appreciated for their decorative qualities. Library ladders, for instance, grant access to shelves that are out of reach; many of them also possess sculptural forms that can enhance a room. Bookstands once stood atop library tables so scholars could ponder a particular page; today they are often placed on a sideboard or hall table to highlight a beautiful illustration. Globes, magnifying glasses, and bookends are but a few examples of useful objects that have become sought-after collectibles.

LIGHTING

After spending considerable time and energy arranging a book collection, you'll want to make sure it is seen in its best light. In a room with ample sunlight, this won't be much of an issue—during the day, at least. In the evening and in dimly lit rooms, sufficient lighting is of the essence. There are a number of ways this can be achieved. Library lamps can be attached directly to the front of a bookcase, just above the top shelf. Small lights can also be recessed along the top, side, or bottom of a shelf. Track lighting installed overhead can illuminate the volumes from above. And wall sconces or freestanding lamps positioned nearby can brighten the general area.

LEFT: The brass light fixtures adorning the top of these bookcases provide ample illumination to the titles neatly stacked on the shelves below. They also coordinate nicely with the other elements around the room—the colors, the crown atop the shelves, the elephant side tables—to create a fun Hollywood-inspired Mediterranean look in this 1920s suburban home.

BELOW: Here, the long brass lamp positioned high above the bookcase floods the display on the top shelf with light and softly illuminates the books on lower shelves. Additional sources of light are especially needed when books are displayed far from a window.

OPPOSITE: To house this family's most beloved books, a special mahogany bookcase was constructed. Each shelf is wrapped in burgundy silk and a formidable Gothic crown molding tops the piece. A brass lamp installed above the shelves illuminates the volumes.

PHOTOGRAPHY CREDITS

Page 1: Tria Giovan **Page 2**: Thibault Jeanson **Page 5**: Laura Resen **Page 6**: Oberto Gili **Page 8**: Thibault Jeanson **Page 10**: Laura Resen **Page 12**: John Coolidge **Page 13**: Oberto Gili **Page 14**: Laura Resen **Page 15**: William Waldron **Page 16**: Jean-Francois Jaussaud **Page 18**: Jacques Dirand **Page 19**: Jacques Dirand **Page 20**: Minh + Wass **Page 21**: Mikkel Vang **Page 22–23**: Scott Frances **Page 23**: Scott Frances **Page 23**: Scott Frances **Page 24**: Luca Trovato **Page 25**: Minh + Wass **Page 26–27**: William Waldron **Page 28**: Buff Strickland **Page 29**: Buff Strickland **Page 29**: Buff Strickland **Page 30**: Paul Wicheloe **Page 31**: Rene Stoeltie **Page 32–33**: Thibault Jeanson **Page 34**: Christopher Baker **Page 35**: Minh + Wass **Page 36**: William Waldron **Page 37**: Thomas Loof **Page 38**: Fernando Bengoechea **Page 39**: Richard Felber **Page 40**: Fernando Bengoechea **Page 41**: Fernando Bengoechea **Page 42**: Steve Freihon **Page 44**: Carlos Emilio **Page 45**: William Waldron **Page 46**: Tim Street-Porter **Page 47**: John Coolidge **Page 48–49**: Oberto Gili **Page 49**: Gordon Beall **Page 50**: John Coolidge **Page 51**: Gordon Beall **Page 52**: Tim Street-Porter **Page 53**: Fernando Bengoechea **Page 54**: Victoria Pearson **Page 55**: John M. Hall **Page 56**: Tim Street-Porter **Page 57**: Gordon Beall **Page 58–59**: Edmund Barr **Page 59**: Andreas von Einsiedel **Page 60**: Laura Resen **Page 61**: Dominique Vorillon **Page 62 (left)**: John Coolidge **Page 62 (right)**: William P. Steele **Page 63**: Jeff McNamara **Page 64**: Tria Giovan **Page 65**: Gordon Beall **Page 66**: Laura Resen **Page 67**: Roger Davies **Page 68**: Evan Sklar **Page 59**: William Waldron **Page 70**: Minh + Wass **Page 72**: Colleen Duffley **Page 73**: Courtesy of *House Beautiful* **Page 74**: Michael O'Brien **Page 75**: John Coolidge **Page 76**: Evan Sklar **Page 77**: Luke White **Page 78**: John M. Hall **Page 79**: Carlos Emilio **Page 80–81**: Fernando Bengoechea **Page 82**: Michael O'Brien **Page 83**: Thibault Jeanson **Page 84**: Jean-Francois Jaussaud **Page 85**: William Waldron **Page 86**: Fernando Bengoechea **Page 87 (left)**: Minh + Wass **Page 87 (right)**: Fernando Bengoechea **Page 88 (left)**: John Coolidge **Page 88 (right)**: Dana Gallagher **Page 89**: Fernando Bengoechea **Page 90**: Gordon Beall **Page 91**: Dana Gallagher **Page 92–93**: John Coolidge **Page 94**: Tim Street-Porter **Page 95**: Rene Stoeltie **Page 96**: Minh + Wass **Page 98**: Oberto Gili **Page 99**: Simon Upton **Page 100**: John M. Hall **Page 101**: Laura Resen **Page 102–103**: John Coolidge **Page 104**: Christopher Simon Sykes **Page 105**: Timothy Hursley **Page 106**: John Coolidge **Page 107**: Fernando Bengoechea **Page 108**: Simon Upton **Page 109**: Simon Upton **Page 110–111**: Erik Kvalsvik **Page 112**: Fernando Bengoechea **Page 113**: Jan Tham **Page 114–115**: Eric Boman **Page 115**: John Coolidge **Page 116**: Eric Piasecki **Page 117**: Eric Piasecki **Page 118**: Jeff McNamara **Page 119**: Tim Street-Porter **Page 120**: Tim Beddow **Page 121**: Oberto Gili **Page 122**: Tim Street-Porter **Page 124**: Thibault Jeanson **Page 125 (left)**: Oberto Gili **Page 125 (right)**: William Waldron **Page 126**: William Waldron **Page 127**: Eric Boman **Page 128**: Toshi Otsuki **Page 129**: Fernando Bengoechea **Page 130**: Tria Giovan **Page 131**: Richard Felber **Page 132**: Courtesy of *Victoria* **Page 133**: Thomas Loof **Page 134**: John M. Hall **Page 135**: Carlos Emilio **Page 136 (left)**: Courtesy of *House Beautiful* **Page 136 (right)**: Laura Resen **Page 137**: William P. Steele **Page 138**: Roger Davies **Page 139 (left)**: Elizabeth Zeschin **Page 139 (right)**: Scott Frances

INDEX